Λ

Carol Ann Duffy is Poet Laureate and Professor of
Contemporary Poetry at Manchester Metropolitan
University, where she is also Creative Director of the
Writing School. Her poetry for both children and adults
has received many awards, most recently the Costa
Poetry Award for *The Bees* (2011). She was awarded the
PEN Pinter Prize in 2012. *Ritual Lighting* (*Laureate
Poems*) was published in 2014, and *The Map and the
Clock*, an anthology covering fourteen centuries of poetry
from across the British Isles, co-curated with Gillian Clarke,
in 2016. Her other work for theatre includes *Grimm
Tales*, *Beasts and Beauties*, *Rats' Tales* and *Everyman*.

Rufus Norris is Director of the National Theatre, where
he recently directed *The Threepenny Opera, wonder.land*
and *Everyman*. He was previously an Associate Director
at the National, directing *Behind the Beautiful Forevers,
The Amen Corner, Table, London Road, Death and the
King's Horseman* and *Market Boy*. Productions elsewhere
include *Feast, Vernon God Little, Peribanez, Hergé's
Adventures of Tintin, Afore Night Come* and *Sleeping
Beauty* for the Young Vic; *Festen* and *Blood Wedding* for
the Almeida; *Under the Blue Sky* and *About the Boy* for
the Royal Court, and many others. His productions of
Cabaret, Festen, Hergé's Adventures of Tintin and *The
Country Girl* have all played in the West End and toured
nationally, and he directed *Les Liaisons Dangereuses* on
Broadway. Opera work includes *Dr Dee* with Damon
Albarn for MIF and ENO, and *Don Giovanni* at ENO. His
debut feature film *Broken* had its premiere at Cannes in
2012; his film of *London Road* was released in June 2015.

CAROL ANN DUFFY
and
RUFUS NORRIS

My Country
A Work in Progress

in the words of people across the UK
and Carol Ann Duffy

FABER & FABER

First published in 2017
by Faber and Faber Limited
74–77 Great Russell Street
London WC1B 3DA

Typeset by Country Setting, Kingsdown, Kent CT14 8ES
Printed in England by CPI Group (UK) Ltd, Croydon CR0 4YY

A CIP record for this book is available from the British Library

ISBN 978–0–571–33974–7

2 4 6 8 10 9 7 5 3 1

My Country was first staged in the Dorfman auditorium of the National Theatre, London, on 28 February 2017, before a national tour. The company, in alphabetical order, was as follows:

East Midlands Seema Bowri
Northern Ireland Cavan Clarke
North-East Laura Elphinstone
South-West Adam Ewan
Britannia Penny Layden
Caledonia Stuart McQuarrie
Cymru Christian Patterson

Director Rufus Norris
Designer Katrina Lindsay
Lighting Designer Paul Knott
Music David Shrubsole
Sound Designer Alex Caplen
Movement Polly Bennett
Creative Producer Pádraig Cusack
Company Voice Work Jeannette Nelson

Interview gatherers:
Sarah Blowers, Gez Casey, Kieran Griffiths, Adam Kent, Campbell Lawrie, Jo Newman, Lindsay Rodden, Sara Shaarawi, Julia Thomas, Rhiannon White

Created in collaboration with: Citizens Theatre, Glasgow; Curve, Leicester; Derry Playhouse; Live Theatre, Newcastle; National Theatre of Wales; Sage Gateshead; Salisbury Playhouse and Strike A Light, in association with Cusack Projects Limited.

MY COUNTRY

in memory of
JO COX MP

THE ARRIVALS

Britannia enters.

Britannia Nice one. You've all turned up. I'm grateful. The others are due any minute. I just – I thought there should be listeners. Witnesses, if you like. I'll get this place sorted. And could you turn your mobiles off? Thanks.

Selects lighting, music, tries on Britannia helmet.
    The regions arrive promptly. During their arrivals Britannia is busily focused on setting up the room for the meeting.
    Caledonia changes music track. Britannia turns off.

Caledonia Got your message.

Britannia Caledonia. Hello.

Caledonia Did ye have to leave the hairdresser's in a hurry?

Britannia It would be nice if I did get some time to spend on myself. I've hardly slept.

Caledonia Poor wee Britney!

Britannia It's good you agreed to come.

Caledonia For the moment, Britney . . . for the moment.
    You love wearing this eh? I remember you in 1603 at the Coronation of James I, we used it as a quaich. The Act of Union 1707, Andrew Fletcher of Saltoun did a jobby in it. (*Sings 'My Little Pony.'*)

Britannia Now look, the last time we met . . .

South-West The Bay City Rollers were at Number One.

Britannia What?

South-West Last time we all met up. 'Bye bye, baby, don't make me cry.' Seventy per cent of the UK voted to join the Common Market. 'Bye bye, baby, don't say goodbye.' 1975.

Caledonia South-West. You nerd.

South-West Reporting for duty, Britney.

Britannia All of our meetings throughout history have been so important to me.

South-West You give me any time we've met and I'll give you the Number One – or its equivalent, because strictly speaking, the Charts as we know them didn't really start until 1952.

Caledonia Second World War.

South-West We met at the start and finish, which do you want?

Caledonia Start.

South-West 1939. Vera Lynn. 'We'll meet again, don't know where, don't know when, but I know . . .'

Caledonia Sinking of the *Titanic*.

South-West 'I'm shy, Mary Ellen, I'm shy, It does seem so naughty, oh my. Kissing is nicey . . .'

Caledonia 1801.The Inclosure Act.

South-West ''Twas in the solemn midnight hour when all was dark around, when planets strike . . .'

Caledonia The Declaration of Arbroath. 1321.

Pause.

Ya beauty!

South-West The Declaration of Arbroath was 1320.

'Ice herde men ups mould make much mon
Hou he beth itened of here tilyynge.'

Song of the Husbandman.

Cymru (*sings*)
'Paham mae dicter, O Myfanwy –'

Caledonia Here's your favourite.

Cymru (*continues*)
'Yn llenwi'th lygaid duon di?
A'th ruddiau tirion, O Myfanwy,
Heb wrido wrth fy ngweled i?'

Britannia Bore da, Cymru.

Cymru Bore da, Britney. You summoned and I came as always, Cariad.

Britannia I can't thank you enough.

Cymru South-West.

South-West How do.

Caledonia Cymru.

Cymru Bluddy thrashed you at the rugby last week, boy.

Caledonia Two words for you, pal. *Andy*. And *Murray*. I'm no hearing the world of tennis is dominated by the Welsh?

Cymru Two words right back at you. *Gareth* and *Bale*.

South-West *Eddie* and *Eagle*.

Britannia Can we get this room sorted?

Cymru Eddie the bluddy Eagle?

5

South-West The most successful of his countrymen at the sport of ski-jumping *bar none*. Born and bred in Gloucestershire.

Caledonia Oh aye. The renowned ski-slopes of Cheltenham.

South-West It's not Cheltenham, it's Matson.

Cymru What?

South-West You can see it from the A417.

Caledonia This is fascinating.

Northern Ireland Hallo!

Britannia Northern Ireland! Thank you *so* much for coming.

Northern Ireland No problem. The Referendum. I wasn't surprised to hear from you.

East Midlands Britannia. These are serious times.

Britannia *Thank you*, East Midlands. *Yes.* Serious times. Once again we find ourselves at a crucial moment in our nation's history. I hope this room's OK. It was all I could get at short notice. And this time, I've invited an audience.

Caledonia So we've tae mind our fuckin language?

Britannia Before witnesses we shall listen to those voices we have gathered and see what we can learn. You are the spirits and hearts of your regions and you honour the voices of your people.

Cymru Don't worry, Britney bach. We won't let you down.

All concur.

Britannia I know that. Er . . . where's North-East?

North-East Sorry I'm late like. Terrible journey, man.

6

Northern Ireland Just off the Jarrow March?

North-East We've had gale-force winds. The Angel of the North is on a tilt. Durham Cathedral looks twatted. Had to change trains twice, upgrade on one, sit in the corridor on the other, then queue jump at the taxi rank . . . Nearly threw up in the taxi 'cause I got absolutely shit-faced the night before . . . I'd learn to drive but I'm nervous of caravans.

Britannia I'd like to call this gathering to order.
    Inter se conveniente Britanniae – the gathering of the family of Britannia in the year 2017 – Her Majesty Queen Elizabeth II being in the sixty-fifth year of her reign. Welcome.

All Welcome.

Britannia (*to audience*) Welcome to all who have journeyed here to listen in this place.
    Present?

Caledonia Caledonia.

South-West South-West.

Cymru Cymru.

Northern Ireland Northern Ireland.

East Midlands East Midlands.

North-East North-East.

Britannia We are convened to meet the matter of this time, and speak verbatim in the voices of our regions. As Britannia, I speak today the words of the leadership at Westminster. Say now for where you speak.

Caledonia I speak today for Glasgow. And for Edinburgh. Twin capitals of Caledonia.

Cymru I speak today for Merthyr Tydfil in the Welsh Valleys.

East Midlands I speak today for Leicester, the centre of England.

South-West I speak today for Salisbury and for Gloucester. Cathedral Cities.

Northern Ireland I speak today for Derry Londonderry. Legenderry.

North-East I speak today for Sunderland, Gateshead, Northumberland, Durham. And South bleedin Shields.

Britannia Say now for whom you speak.

David.

South-West Mila.

Northern Ireland Sean.

North-East Terry.

Caledonia James.

East Midlands Aravinda.

Cymru Paul.

Britannia Listen.

South-West Jane.

Northern Ireland Siobhan.

North-East Carlos.

Caledonia Carol.

East Midlands TJ.

Cymru Dafydd.

Britannia Boris.

South-West Eddie.

Northern Ireland Luke.

North-East Jasper.

Caledonia Adam.

East Midlands Stu.

Cymru Pauline.

Britannia
  Listen . . .

South-West Stanley.

Northern Ireland Mick.

North-East Roxie.

Caledonia Roseanne.

East Midlands Julie.

Cymru Matthew.

Britannia Michael.

South-West Beryl.

Northern Ireland Declan.

North-East Jude.

Caledonia Glenn.

East Midlands May.

Cymru Jonathan.

Britannia Nigel.

South-West Olly.

Northern Ireland Richard.

North-East Bill.

Caledonia Padma.

East Midlands Lee.

Cymru Amanda.

Britannia Jeremy.

South-West Leroy.

Northern Ireland Niamh.

North-East Barbara.

Caledonia Deirdre.

East Midlands Maureen.

Cymru Bernice.

Britannia Jo.

South-West Ella.

Northern Ireland Des.

North-East Jackie.

Caledonia Andrew.

East Midlands Eric.

Cymru Curtis.

Britannia Theresa.

South-West Joanne.

Northern Ireland Mick.

North-East Larry.

Caledonia Lenny.

East Midlands Donna.

Cymru Angharad.

Britannia
So.
Listen to me and let me hear your words:
not to agree, but – as the song of birds
reveals the light,

the darkness lessening –
to hear this human music; silence loosening
within the Sacrament of Listening.

All The Sacrament of Listening.

Britannia I move to the Opening Voices. Verbatim.

THE SIX ARIAS

Caledonia (*William*) When I used to go to school, we'd
look at . . . Fettes over the road wi its massive sweepin
driveway . . . and the castle thàt we used to call Castle
Duckula . . . You know frae the show? *Count Duckula,*
yeah? An, an from my school we didn't, we couldn't
afford a swimming pool. We got sent to the Victorian
swimming pool that was within grounds of Fettes
Academy . . . Y'know? An we really got to see how the
other side of the tracks got taught. You know? An right
from the start and eve— huh, even more so when they
explained tae me that ma school was actually owned by
their school. That ma school, the council just rented it
from them. And that they also rent the Police Headquarters
land and right the way up to where Telford College used
to be. That's all owned by Fettes School. And you can't
buy any land on that land. You can only lease it for
ninety-nine years and then it reverts back to Castle
Duckula on the hill. And yet the fees for that school were
some of the highest in the whole of the UK. And you see
them aw troopin out in their nice academy uniforms
wearing Harris Tweed jackets, ken what I mean? And
they walk past aw – ay – us scheemies. And they got
different times tae come out of school so they would
never interact with us and the boarding school thur . . .
They would come out and they would literally buy two
big bags of sweeties and their stuff ken to get them
through the week or whatever. Now I'm no sayin that

these kids were any happier or any . . . b— You know . . .
I'm just sayin that they are set up. They are taught that
money just brings opportunities and that value of life.
Whereas our school over the road were always kinda just
sorta subconsciously told . . . they're the masters.

North-East (*Barbara*) Well, I was actually born on a
farm er, in, er, at Ottercaps, which is just down from
Otterburn, er, so it, my dad was a tenant farmer . . . and
I just from day one I loved the farm really so . . . er . . .
and so I followed my dad about when I could! And er, w-
w— they had three ponies, they had about t-twelve
hundred Swaledale ewes, and we had about maybe sixty-
odd, er, suckler cows and they were Galloways when I
was little and then they became Blue Greys as trends
changed. Everything changed . . . when we started we
were shepherding on ponies. So now it's motorbike and
the dog . . . dog skills definitely dropped. People don't
even have dogs now on some farms which I find incredible.
The whole thing is geared up to big business. I know that
on the hills you don't go shepherding every day any
more, you just go round and you pick up the dead and
that is how it is and the sheep, they're astonished when
you arrive, where as a shepherd in my time they, they
know they know you.

Cymru (*Amanda*) People are very quick to judge. I'm –
I'm – I'm very judgemental, I – I will say that. But I think
. . . more so I've opened my mind since I left the police.
An technically aven't got a job. I don't feel the same. Ah,
how can I explain it? Like, when I ad a – when I was in
the police, not big-eaded or anything, but I was like 'I'm
a police officer.' Now I'm nothin. I'm nothin . . . an it's
wrong, because you don't know people's backgrounds . . .
especially like when you got th— the homeless is a big
thing . . . people automatically assume the homeless are
druggies and alkies and they're not. And I'm one of them,

I'm guilty of that. But I've, I've, and it was a trip it was a night out in Cardiff actually that made me change my mind . . . cos we offered these people some food and they said 'Oh no thank you we've eaten,' they weren't drunk, they weren't on drugs, and they didn't . . . they weren't scrounging . . . they were just like 'Oh a hot drink would be lovely,' and that's changed my mindset about people in general altogether, not to like judge straight away. But the one thing that gripes me is – and I've ad first-hand experience of it – is a friend – who I took my house off the market for, to rent to her, with er children – she owes me two grand in rent. And she stole my settees. And when I worked out how much benefit she was getting in a month, she was getting in benefits – and that was without her council tax *and* her housing allowance – *more* than what I was takin home as a police officer. An that really grips my shit.

Northern Ireland (*Declan*) I think – I think I had, em – I had a moment. I wouldn't say it was one of my defining moments, but I had a time – I remember sittin watchin TV with my sister and Jason Donovan was on. And it was clearly like, you know, the late eighties an . . . I looked at the TV an she was sitting in the armchair beside the window and I was sitting on the floor, em, by the fireplace and he was on and I said, 'He's a babe.' You know? And she looked down at me and she said, 'You're not supposed to say things like that.'

I was three, she was eleven, you know, – there was eight years between us. Em, there still are eight years between us! (*Laughs.*)

And eh – you know, at that point, I knew I was different because I wasn't just saying words for the sake of saying words – I fucking meant it! I fancied the man on the TV and I was a tot. You know, and lookin back, in hindsight, it's a moment that – again – em, had an impact on me. Em, and it's just part of the journey.

East Midlands (*Aravinda*) I was coming to the land of milk and honey! But uhh . . . there's no . . . there's milk. I can buy for a pound two litres of milk. I can buy a jar of honey for a pound. You know I'm . . . uh, happy and um . . . if you like, grateful 'cause er . . . they gave me opportunity to earn money, they gave me opportunity to raise my family . . . they gave me opportunity to own my own home and uhh . . . you know, all the health, you know, National Health and all that there for me to benefit if I fall ill, uhh . . . But it's not a land of milk and honey. It's not that heaven that all the immigrants think it is. It's not.

South-West (*Jane*) Twenty happy years in Bristol. But, you know, big city, and you feel it's time to um, well quite literally this was my escape to the country. (*Laughs.*) We are, the baby boom's generation, you know, we are the, you know I was born in 1947, Brian was born in 1944, you know, so yes, you know, we have lived this life where we've seen many, many changes . . . OK I'm a lucky lady, look at me, I'm middle class you know and I've got a good good man, who has you know, made a beautiful home for us, you know, I'm very very conventional. We've always you know been, I don't know if cocooned is the right word . . . but you know, we've worked hard, it's not just fallen into our laps . . . so I've been to the children's parents' evenings and I've been to the children's plays and all that sort of thing because he has done nothing but work *but* he's given us all this . . . Had twelve very happy years in Plymouth, brilliant place to bring up the children, you know, it was either going to the beach or going up on Dartmoor or going to Plymbridge Woods and you can guarantee I always brought somebody home wet! It was either a child or the dog! I've never ever had any sort of um . . . great stress in my life, you know, because I've had a good man and a lovely home and a lovely family, you know all the brothers and sisters and

uncles and aunts. OK I'm one of the lucky ones . . . um . . .
but I've still contributed to society, you know, I've taught
children, you know, there's some children out there who
probably still remember Mrs Sandells.

Britannia Thank you.

Let us be closer. And now we will hear the story in this
time, in the people's words. The instigating voice is
David.

THE VOICES: EUROPE

Britannia (*Cameron*) We are approaching one of the
biggest decisions this country will face in our lifetimes.
Whether to remain in a reformed European Union – or to
leave. The choice goes to the heart of the kind of country
we want to be . . . We will give the British people a
referendum with a very simple in or out choice. We will
give the British people a referendum lock, to which only
they should hold the key.

North-East (*Bill*) Thi— this is what sums up the EU to
me, the EU is like . . . an older sibling who's on the dole,
right, and it comes to ya birthday present and you're . . .
ten years old, and your brother bought ya a Scalextric
and you go wow! Thanks brother! Scalextric, just what
I wanted! But really, your mother has paid for it,

South-West (*Douglas*) I, I sense that the countries of
Europe are less, um, passionate about their borders and
their flag and so on, than we are, 'cause we're an island
nation, and it's, it's, remarkable, it seems to me what a
difference it makes if your boundaries are water.

Britannia (*Cameron*) We have the character of an island
nation – independent, forthright, passionate in defence of
our sovereignty.

Cymru (*Marta*) And I think where European Union had a like a bigger picture they say 'Right, there is a area, they poor, they need, we need to do something here, we need to build . . . when I used to cycle around like Brecon . . . Brecon to Cardiff I used to cycle, and you come across and there is a canal and it says 'This was rebuilded because European Union money donated there.'

Northern Ireland (*Mick*) Underpriviliged and deprived areas were benefiting from the EU programme. Ah . . . maybe not to such a degree as I would like – like tae see. But that it was happening . . .

South-West (*Jane*) We have sent them billions. And when you see what has happened to Brussels it has all been completely redeveloped . . . Just go outside Eurostar station and you are in the middle of the most amazing plaza . . . huge modern buildings . . .

Northern Ireland (*Niamh*) The EU doesn't work. It's one size fits all and we're not one size fits all we're different countries with different histories, different cultures, different er . . . personalities.

Caledonia (*Andrew*) We're kinda, almost double-ruled in Scotland because you've got the flow from the EU which comes through UK and then the rules which the UK Government make which then impact on Scotland.

Britannia (*Cameron*) But we will be safer and stronger and better off working together in a reformed Europe.

Cymru (*Angharad*) Britain ave always been er, a country that's a self-sufficient. We nev— we weren't in the European Union whe-when the war was on and things like this and we were self-sufficient then, we fed our families an kept clothes and roofs above our 'eads so . . . my answer is still why do we ave to go to the European Union for anything for them to say yay or nay.

Northern Ireland (*Niamh*) Generally speaking, if you give us a law, we'll obey it. You give a law to a Greek or to a Spaniard or to a Frenchman he'll say yeah yeah and he might implement half of it or he might not, he won't worry about it. I was in Barcelona and I was up on one of those Gaudi buildings and we were on the roof and we were walking on an undulating roof and there was not a hand-rail.

East Midlands (*Panit*) Every day there's an idiot from Brussels, you can't do this, you must do this, you must do this, you can't – guys, it's very easy if you're sitting in Brussels creating these *policies* but when you look at the people on the ground, the businessmen, it doesn't work for all of us.

South-West (*Eddie*) I want *us* makin our decisions for *our* country. I don't give a shit if my banana's straight or bent.

Northern Ireland (*Desmond*) Bananas must be like that and not like that.

South-West (*Eddie*) I don't give a shit if it's green or orange, my orange, you know, it can be green if it's soft, it's fine, I don't care, who cares . . .

East Midlands (*May*) They wanted to make our mushy peas become . . . you couldn't put the green in it. What?!

South-West (*Eddie*) I had a green banana in Kenya and it was soft, so why's it gotta be yellow, you know, in Kenya it was green but soft, that's amazing isn't it! Get one over here, it's solid! So how does that work?

Britannia (*Boris*) If, if, I tell you what, if the EU were an animal I tell you what it would be, it would be a lobster. Because the EU, by the very way it works, encourages its participating members to order the lobster at the joint meal, because they know the bill is going to be settled by everybody else. So that's what the EU would be, it would be a gigantic lobster with a, with a erm, butter sauce or something like that.

North-East (*Larry*) Er say eight, nine year old, I just used to hop on the local bus and go to Warkworth and then just walk the – walk the mile to the r— eh, to the river and just spend all day fishin. Like at one time, I remember when I was er – younger, th-they'd . . . that – in Amble harbour, the boats were three and four abreast all the way along the harbour. Now you're lucky if there's one line of boats up against the pier now. And for every, for every, for every man that was – that was on a boat, there was six jobs ashore. So if you had – if you had five men on a boat, that's five sixes, that's thirty odd . . . per boat! Eh, the, the thing is, if we took our waters back – now any – any boat from anywhere around the world from what I gather, can come here and fish twelve mile off our shore. Seventy per cent of the fish they catch is – is in our waters, which to me is totally wrong. Hopefully we wanna get out the EU, en, en, en take – take wer water back. Jus take – take wer water back, they shouldn't be allowed to come and fish our waters, they should fish their own. You're like, we're governed – the net sizes, fish sizes . . . we have to . . . our fish has to be pristine, it has to be put on ice. Them lot – it's just thrown in the baskets. The EU's wrecked the fishing industry . . .

THE VOICES: PATRIOTISM

Britannia (*Cameron*) We all know what's wrong with the EU – it's got too big, too bossy, too interfering. Believe me, I have no romantic attachment to the European Union and its institutions. I will never say that our country couldn't survive outside Europe.

I do not love Brussels. I love Britain.

East Midlands (*Panit*) It's Great Britain because the words mean something.

Caledonia (*Lenny*) I've never felt British. Really. Never. I'm proudly Glaswegian.

Northern Ireland (*Niamh*) I got an Irish passport because I'm Irish!

North-East (*Larry*) I'm English en-en-en proud of it. Just because the way we are en er, en-en-en-en wer traditions.

South-West (*Jane*) Being British is something I'm very, very proud of.

Caledonia (*Andrew*) I really think Scotland should be in charge of everything and govern itself.

South-West (*Jane*) We grew up thi— thinking we were the best country in the world, you know, we're tolerant of gays, we're tolerant of um um race . . .

Britannia (*Cameron*) I'm a deeply patriotic person about this country. We have not been invaded for a thousand years.

East Midlands (*Donna*) And at the end of the day we've got Queen, Queen and country.

Northern Ireland (*Richard*) I love the British connection, the tradition, but I'm not a big Queen person. Britain doesn't want us. Who does want us? Nobody wants us. They've only held on to us because they know no one else wants us. If they cut us adrift there'd be a few pound more in their pockets. We've nothing to give apart from history of troubles. I don't think there should be flags flown at sporting events, or national anthems. They're divisive.

North-East (*Chris*) It feels like all these marches where you've got, like the erm, EDL with the, with the, with their St George, the *English* St George, it's not Great Britain – Union Jacks – that I . . . I dunno whe— er, I went down the shops and that it was kind of rammed when the football was on and everyone had flags hanging out the windows and I looked at them flags . . . and I thought I don't feel part of that.

Cymru (*Curtis*) Curtis Thomas Popp. Thirteen years old. I live in Merthyr Tydfil and I was born in 2003 and that's it. I wanna support my country. Oh it's amazing, you sh-should um . . . you should come and ave er . . . a look at the sights. You get good – you get good people running stores, you get good friends here, you get good schools, you get good – train service, you get good bus service, you get, um, good taxi service. Yoooou get good town, you get good sh— you get good shopping centres, you get good – beaches – and you get a good scenery and that's it . . . I am in the Royal Navy cadets, R-Royal Air Force cadets and I wanna support my country.

Northern Ireland (*Mick*) The British Army raided our house. There was a shootin incident – let's say it – put it that way, away down around the Brandywell or somethin ye know and – eh . . . Maybe about two hours after it, I was sittin in the house. And eh – I was sittin in the armchair and they came in the – our house was a bar, as well, right ye know so – so everything was fucking sealed down, ye know, and nobody's allowed tae move – they're all up the stairs and down the stairs and eh . . . eventually this Major eh – he was Major Stackpoll, that's how he was – you'd call him. He looked in at the door an he looked over at me an he says, 'Michael.' (*Laughs.*) A big fancy English accent . . . He says, 'I don't like you; I don't like any of your friends; I don't like any of your associates and I'll get you.' (*Laughs.*) And he turned and walked out!

Britannia (*Farage*) We are unashamedly the patriotic party.

It's about priorities, isn't it, and my priority would be we put our own people first.

There's an issue called the quality of life.

The gap between rich and poor is getting bigger and bigger and bigger. We've been through a decade now where for people earning average salaries they're ten per cent worse off than they were back in 2007. That simply can't be right.

THE VOICES: HARDSHIP

Cymru (*Angharad*) Live in my world for six months. Come and live like I ave to. Fetching up a family you know wanting to go back to work and I can't because I'm not well enough. Come an live as I'm living with the money you're telling me to live on. You don't get no airs, you don't get no graces that is what you live on every week.

Caledonia (*William*) We've only got six million people up here. And you go round – you go through Fife where the whole industry used to employ the whole village. And that industry died. So that whole village now doesnae have a main industry.

North-East (*Terry*) I think the biggest change is when the, the number of people that's left and eh – what's happened is the, the numbered streets have – have, have, eh – have emptied.

Caledonia (*William*) So the parents that live there, they're watchin their kids grown up and goin 'You don't have any opportunities here.'

North-East (*Terry*) The football club's that's disbanded now, er, the rugby club's moved to Peterlee 'cause they can't pay the, 'cause they, they the rent's too too big and all that so.

Caledonia (*William*) So they kids have tae move – they move to America, Canada, J-Japan, London. Any-fuckin-where. Because there's nothin in Scotland.

Britannia (*Boris*) The harder you shake the pack, the easier it will be for some cornflakes to get to the top. I stress: I don't believe that economic equality is possible; indeed, some measure of inequality is essential for the spirit of envy and keeping up with the Joneses and so on, that is a valuable spur to economic activity.

North-East (*Jude*) The way erm, that they treat the ordinary people who maybe have worked all their lives and for no, no fault of their own have been made redundant or, you know, something's closed down or they've been finished and they're tret like second-class citizens when they've paid tax all their lives . . .

East Midlands (*Julie*) I never thought as a worker you can still struggle. So sometimes I had to decide if I'm payin ten pounds to put in my car for petrol or buying food. Which are you gonna pick?

Britannia (*Boris*) To get back to my cornflake packet, I worry that there are too many cornflakes who aren't being given a good enough chance to rustle and hustle their way to the top.

East Midlands (*Julie*) I was living on forty-five pounds a week. And I went and, and I said, 'I can't go to work because I'm on crutches. I need some help,' and I was like 'I've been working,' I says, 'I've been working from the time I could work and earn money, I've been working.' I says, 'Can't you help me?' And he went, 'No. We can't help you.' And I said 'But – I've paid in' – so my heart went. And then next to me, you know, they were from Somalia and they came through Belgium? If you come from a certain way, they can automatically get benefits this side and somewhere to live at the time? And he says, 'Oh, my daughter's come.' Via Belgium – they know the spiel, what to say. And he's saying, 'Yeah, no problem. Here's a cheque for so and so, and you'll have accommodation for three bedrooms – because you say your wife is comin as well. You should hear from us in the next two or three weeks.' And I'm there in tears on crutches.

THE VOICES: IMMIGRATION

Britannia (*Farage*) Look, whichever way you cut this, immigration is the number one issue in British politics, it has been for some years and the opinion polls are astonishing. Seventy-seven per cent of the British public want cuts to the numbers coming into Britain and over half the voters want a reduction to near zero . . . They're seeing the impact on local schools, they're seeing the impact on GP services, they're seeing the impact on housing . . . so people are very upset, they're very unhappy.

Caledonia (*Mary*) I've no got a problem with immigration –

North-East (*Larry*) Now I'm not against immigration –

South-West (*Ralph*) It doesn't affect me, immigration . . .

Caledonia (*Mary*) – but right now there's too many heading to the UK,

North-East (*Larry*) – because of wor benefits system, but we cannet not give anybody that comes here benefits because of the EU.

South-West (*Ralph*) It makes me wealthy, immigration, cos it's pushed up all the house prices and it's made jobs easier, it's kept the wages down of my staff.

Cymru (*Jonathan*) Last couple of years gone crazy like people coming over here to claim benefits –

Northern Ireland (*Desmond*) All the foreigners that are coming from all the countries –

Cymru (*Jonathan*) India, Pakistan –

Northern Ireland (*Desmond*) Romania, Bulgaria –

Cymru (*Jonathan*) Portuguese, Polish, like I get on with a lot of the Polish I don't mind them –

Caledonia (*Mary*) Romanians, Slovakians, Bulgarians –

Cymru (*Jonathan*) All 'em poor countries, cos they can get benefits, cos we're seen as a soft target.

Northern Ireland (*Desmond*) Lookin for work.

Cymru (*Jonathan*) I know there's people that's claiming for kids that don't even live in this country. It's like murderers and rapists from other countries. Pisses me off. Pisses me off big time. We just had some of them Syrians coming here.

North-East (*Jude*) I just ff— think I, well . . . I hate seeing any, seeing all these people in Syria, all these children and . . . I would have one, I would have one 'morrow in a heartbeat. I would have a family if I could . . . and I think we're dreadful that we should turn our noses up to these people and say, we don't want you and you can't come and I think it's *horrible* and they should be mortally ashamed of themselves.

Cymru (*Matthew*) They complaining about Syrians, well why would you want to stay in Syria right now? Y'know with the UK and America bombing you. You know, you're sick. Y'know, if, if you gonna bomb a country expect . . . if you're gonna ex– export bombs you're gonna import people aren't you so.

Caledonia (*Glenn*) I'd – I'd open the doors to all of them, quite frankly.

South-West (*Beryl*) There's good and bad in everyone. Um, I got loads of people who are like, um, yeah, different colours. I'm on the Chinese women's guild, I'm on the Saint Anne's – Uh, yeah, um, I love em all. At the end of the day we all got a front door and a back door haven't we. We're all the same. We all got' pull our pants up and down. Queen an' all.

Britannia (*Cameron*) Yes, we have got, I think, the most successful multi-racial multi-ethnic democracy on Earth, it's a matter of huge pride to people in this country, huge pride to me.

Caledonia (*Andrew*) The poverty that some of those people are living in, the conditions that they're living in . . . and the fact that a lot of them can't speak English, and don't have that support or help there to be able to learn or speak English, is quite a dangerous thing . . . One of the local schools that I was in quite recently, has . . . 310 pupils . . . and thirty-two different languages are spoken in that school . . . and when I said to the head teacher you know . . . 'H-how do you how do you educate thirty-two different languages?' she said 'I can't, I have no physical possible way of doing that, we need to muddle through, on a daily basis . . .'
   Some of the flats I go into have . . . ten . . . sometimes fifteen people living in one flat . . . Went into a flat in Govanhill . . . er, quite recently for a man with chest pain and when we switched the lights on in the living room, the cockroaches . . . ran up the walls and across the couch, across the bed that had kids sleepin in the bed in the living room, and you know the . . . It, it's just not right, it's completely wrong. So . . . if every household has come here for some something different, whether, it be safety from war or . . . economic benefits, you know

they've all got different reasons for being in Scotland or being in Glasgow. But they aren't really integrating with other communities or with the wider community.. And I think that's a very dangerous thing to do . . .

North-East (*Larry*) There's so many coming, they're not integrating with people. They're, ya nar, they're offended by what we do and wah we wah different things like Christmases and other celebrations – ye nar, it all offends them, but so why why why come here then, you have to respect your host nation.

Caledonia (*Andrew*) These people need to *want* to be part of the community.

North-East (*Larry*) Like if I, if I, if I moved to another country I – you would have to abide by tha rules.

East Midlands (*Aravinda*) I don't go out of the way to, to be um, imposing my own values on other people you know, I respect and take part in Christmas, I share in the values of the country I'm living in, share the happy times and the sad times.

South-West (*Stanley*) There are no Christian churches in Saudi Arabia, but when they come here, they're allowed mosques . . .

East Midlands (*Aravinda*) Refugee you give him job, he's not appreciating, he wants to bring his own law. If someone's life is in danger, genuine danger, you say yes, but they're lying . . . they're coming with lies and then if you don't agree with them, they going to say, oh no we don't believe in your Jesus . . . my flag black flag will fly on your house, on your Parliament, on your Queen's house.

South-West (*Mila*) There's loads of terrorists around here, well we heard on the news that terrorists are coming into Wiltshire and stuff, but I haven't seen any, so I'm not sure if that's true, but like, because it's the news, you might believe it, but like, some things on the news you can't believe because, like the weather, it says it might rain, but it doesn't.

East Midlands (*Aravinda*) It's the people who do the preaching, preachers, they are putting poison in us. They say 'Oh you will go to Heaven, you'll be martyrs, you'll meet beauty queen there who will marry you.' And I got no time for that sort of thing.

South-West (*Eddie*) I don't agree with things like the burka and all that. You know like totally slit like this. No no no you're walkin round with a balaclava on your head. 'S not a burka, it's a balaclava. You come to this country to better yourself. If you want to take that off an' let your hair down, you do that. You wanna wear a bit a' lippy, you wear a bit a' lippy. You can better yourself.

East Midlands (*Aravinda*) People who put a bomb under somebody's police car, shoot innocent people sitting enjoying a lunch or coffee, where did this poison come from?

Northern Ireland (*Desmond*) Every day there is something wrong, like them I.S. fellas out abroad that have been killing people er, er, and they are doing it for this Allah and all that kinda carry on. I don't know what all that's about.

Caledonia (*William*) Muslims, the Muslim minority just happen to be one of the richest, hardest working sections of our society. Funnily enough they don't believe in banking, lending money. Even though it says that in our Bible, never a lender nor a borrower be, but they actually stick to their principles. And that's fucking scary for all these bankers, because they dinnae want to bank with you.

North-East (*Terry*) I have no problem with people coming in, I mean there's loadsa Polish people in my work my shift en they're, en they're great, I have no problem like.

South-West (*Jane*) People do feel swamped.

East Midlands (*Donna*) It's more um *immigrant* now, yeah . . . in the last . . . forty years, I suppose?

Britannia (*Farage*) The very fact that last year, twenty thousand illegal immigrants were given permanent leave to remain, is it any wonder that a boat was found off Hastings this morning with people in it . . .

East Midlands (*Donna*) Yeah, it's just, all, it's just Asians en Muslims en . . . few whites left.

South-West (*Jane*) If you live in Peterborough, Boston, all these small communities have been overwhelmed by immigrant labour.

East Midlands (*Donna*) You don't feel as safe in the city as you used to –

Northern Ireland (*Desmond*) Seventy-five million now in Britain –

East Midlands (*Donna*) – because obviously there's people around –

Northern Ireland (*Desmond*) – and most of them –

East Midlands (*Donna*) – that haven't been here before and um . . .

Northern Ireland (*Desmond*) – are foreign . . .

East Midlands (*Donna*) Um, you don't sort of see enough of your own people, OK, yes I'm in the wrong area but it would be nice just to see some of your own people more often than you see of other races. Whereas if you go down to the seaside or go down south or somethin you know, then you're with your own a bit more. And it's – there's nothing wrong with that. Because the area that I'm in, we are, we are isolated, there's about three families, but you do feel isolated.

Cymru (*Matthew*) I *prefer* a more diverse community, and y'know, peop— people complain . . .

East Midlands (*Donna*) I don't feel safe because as you walk by them, 'Hello lady' and I th— you know, and I'm thinking I'm not your lady. But I just walk on. You know, and . . . it makes me, uh, it makes me feel angry . . .

Cymru (*Matthew*) Like, without all this diversity we wouldn't have half the things we like . . .

East Midlands (*Donna*) And when I think of what my father and forefathers fought for . . . and what they went through to *survive* and then we get the country that we, we, that we had . . . Taking over everything, uh, and you just see the country going down . . . you see your cities going down, you see the housing going down, there's trouble at schools and we're made out to be the bad guys . . .

Cymru (*Matthew*) It's a thing I heard before is like –

East Midlands (*Donna*) I'm not a bad person.

Cymru (*Matthew*) – the typical guy who complains about immigration. 'There's too many Indians, there's too many . . .' whatever, whatever 'too many of this', right, yet that's the same guy who will go to a pub drink a French lager . . . Go out then, go an ave an Indian, you know, and en go home to his Swedish wife an . . .

East Midlands (*Donna*) It really gets to ya, really gets to ya . . . you know it's just, the people above you in general, if they they, if we speak out, we're racist . . .

Northern Ireland (*Niamh*) What is the worst insult that you can throw at a person in today's society? It used to be that you're a slut . . . that means nothing any more, the worst insult that you can say to someone is you're a racist.

Caledonia (*William*) If you're blue you hate red –

East Midlands (*Donna*) Straight the way you're downtrodden.

Caledonia (*William*) If you're Protestant you hate Catholic –

East Midlands (*Donna*) You're tried to be made to feel guilty.

Caledonia (*William*) If it's poor you hate the rich.

East Midlands (*Donna*) I don't feel guilty.

Caledonia (*William*) If it's Rangers you hate Celtic.

East Midlands (*Donna*) I've lived in it.

Caledonia (*William*) It all works on Otherism.

East Midlands (*Donna*) I see it every day.

Caledonia (*William*) And when there's enough others to blame, then the majority's quite happy, aren't they?

East Midlands (*Donna*) I've seen it for years.

Caledonia (*William*) More and more fear – more and more blame, takin over the media, takin over the newspapers and punting Otherism.

East Midlands (*Donna*) When you get – such as you see in people like they're near enough tramps to look at and you're thinking wh— what are you doing in my country? Why are you demoralising it?

Caledonia (*William*) Otherism. All the way.

East Midlands (*Donna*) This is England.

Cymru (*Fiona and Rhian*) It's not like this is my country!

North-East (*Larry*) It's nobody else's country.

Cymru (*Fiona and Rhian*) This is not your country.

East Midlands (*Donna*) THIS IS MY COUNTRY.

Cymru (*Fiona and Rhian*) Put a big stamp on it!

East Midlands (*Donna*) And if I had to I'd fight for it.

Northern Ireland (*Siobhan*) Fuck me, this is fucking terrifying.

Caledonia (*William*) And what, you're fucking surprised now that society's fractured apart?

North-East (*Barbara*) Er, I was ashamed, now I'm absolutely disgusted by our country.

South-West (*Eddie*) Fucked up. In a word.

THE VOICES: LISTENING AND LEADERSHIP

Britannia (*Cameron*) England, Scotland, Wales, Northern Ireland, we are one people in one union and everyone here can be proud of that. We need to listen to what the people want.

North-East (*Barbara*) They don't listen to anybody.

East Midlands (*Julie*) They do that every time. Instead of talking to the people, you know what, you need to listen to you a bit more.

Britannia (*Gove*) I think the people in this country have had enough of experts.
   I'm not asking the people to trust us. I'm asking them to trust themselves.

East Midlands (*Julie*) They not listen.

Cymru (*Angharad*) No one's listening to me. No one cares what I want.

North-East (*Larry*) I just think that their voices are not being heard, and, and they'll only realise it and they'll only see it when it's too late.

East Midlands (*Julie*) They listen till they get in, and they twist it to how they want to.

Britannia (*Boris*) My friends, it is a stitch-up, it is a stitch-up, indeed it is a, it is the biggest, it is the biggest stitch-up since the Bayeux tapestry.

Caledonia (*Padma*) But we're still not heard . . .

East Midlands (*Julie*) Be honest with us.

Britannia (*Boris*) Knickers to the pessimists. How about that? Let's say knickers to the pessimists. Knickers to all those who talk, all those who talk Britain down, all those who talk Britain down. Let's take back control.

Northern Ireland (*Mick*) The, the stuff that they were comin out wae was absolutely you know, I – I was just – there's – nonsensical.

Britannia (*Cameron*) I know the system is unfair.

Cymru (*Curtis*) If I was the prime minister, I will set a good – a good person to the whole community –

Britannia (*Cameron*) I know you want this answered, but nothing comes easy.

Cymru (*Curtis*) Someone you can trust.

South-West (*Ralph*) I've met a lot of politicians.

Britannia (*Cameron*) Other parties preach to you about a brave new world. We understand that you have to start with the real world and make it better.

South-West (*Ralph*) They all talk absolute shit, frankly.

Cymru (*Curtis*) Try and look after the community.

Caledonia (*Adam*) Cameron's just sold Britain down the river.

Northern Ireland (*Desmond*) He used to think he was listened to, but he wasn't and he mucked up himself then, didn't he?

Britannia (*Cameron*) People are frustrated.

Cymru (*Curtis*) Be kind to the community.

North-East (*Bill*) He's obviously cocked up.

Britannia (*Cameron*) And I am frustrated by this.

Cymru (*Curtis*) Don't be cross about the community.

South-West (*James*) Destroying any shred of decency and honesty and credibility.

Britannia (*Cameron*) Of course I share that frustration.

Caledonia (*William*) Politicians don't give a fuck about people.

Northern Ireland (*Richard*) They can't see the big picture.

Caledonia (*William*) All they actually want people to do is make money until they're sixty-five then die as quickly as possible.

Northern Ireland (*Richard*) They can only see their own side.

Caledonia (*William*) Every wage packet they ever got, they paid . . . *tax* –
    Everythin they ever bought they paid . . . *tax* –
    Everything they ever saved, they paid . . . *tax* –
    And then when they died and they wanted to give it to their fuckin loved ones . . . They *taxed* that as well.

South-West (*Eddie*) I haven't got a lot of time for them.

Caledonia (*William*) Let's all, let's never forget, disnae matter what a politician says tae get intae power. All they actually want *is* power.

Northern Ireland (*Richard*) They don't have the balls to stand up, y'know, for what they really know in their own mind is the right thing to do.

Britannia (*Cameron*) For me this is personal, I came into politics because I believe deeply in public service.

Caledonia (*William*) And the House ay Commons is the best fuckin party in the country by the way.

There's a free bar underneath the camera . . . and we're no talking just alcohol here, we're no talking that. If you want a whisky it's the House of Commons whisky. Distilled specially for the House of Commons.

Cymru (*Curtis*) Be happy.

Caledonia (*William*) It's the best fucking club in town, and it's all free. Ye get a free car –

Northern Ireland Lies.

Caledonia (*William*) Ye get a free house –

Northern Ireland Lies.

Caledonia (*William*) Ye get a free fucking hundred and twenty grand a year.

Cymru (*Curtis*) Have a big smile on your face.

Britannia (*Boris*) This is like the jailer has accidently left the door of the jail open –

South-West (*Eddie*) Hang on . . .

Britannia (*Boris*) – and the people can see the sunlit land beyond.

Caledonia (*William*) Wah, wah, wah . . .

South-West (*Eddie*) We need politicians, I understand that –

North-East (*Larry*) Ah diva know.

South-West (*Eddie*) – but you watch them on the telly . . . they stand there –

Caledonia (*William*) What do they do, stand there . . .

South-West (*Eddie*) – and they're all jeering and laughing, these are serious questions –

Britannia (*Cameron*) I am being completely frank with people.

Caledonia (*William*) Wah wah wah wanker wah wah . . .

Cymru (*Curtis*) Don't be naughty.

South-West (*Eddie*) Urgh urgh right honourable gentleman . . .

East Midlands (*Julie*) What?

Cymru (*Curtis*) Don't be horrid.

North-East (*Barbara*) Talking like a ten-year-old.

Britannia (*Gove*) People need to hear the arguments.

East Midlands (*Julie*) I don't listen to them.

Britannia (*Gove*) Free speech.

Caledonia (*Joshua*) Yeah?

Britannia (*Gove*) Robust debate.

South-West (*Eddie*) He's not a right honourable gentleman.

North-East (*Bill*) Those knackers.

Cymru (*Curtis*) Don't.

Britannia (*Gove*) I don't think that we politicians should mark our own homework.

South-West (*Eddie*) It's all this past history crap innit.

East Midlands (*Lee*) Muppet.

Northern Ireland (*Siobhan*) Shower of wankers.

Cymru (*Curtis*) Don't.

Britannia (*Boris*) Invertebrate jellies.

North-East (*Larry*) Full of shit.

South-West (*Eddie*) Toerag.

Caledonia (*William*) And this is democracy.

North-East (*Barbara*) It's nasty and vicious.

Cymru (*Curtis*) Don't.

Britannia (*Boris*) My policy on cake is pro having it . . . and pro eating it.

Caledonia (*William*) Where is it?

South-West (*Eddie*) Boom.

Cymru (*Curtis*) Don't.

East Midlands (*Maureen*) Crumbs.

North-East (*Jude*) Absolute twit.

Britannia (*Farage*) The idea that people are disconnected from politics is wrong.

Caledonia (*William*) Fucking –

Northern Ireland (*Mick*) Politics is corruption.

Caledonia (*William*) – idiot.

Cymru (*Curtis*) Don't.

Britannia (*Farage*) People are not disconnected from politics, they are disconnected from politicians.

East Midlands (*Julie*) Are you serious?

Northern Ireland (*Declan*) Stupid people.

South-West (*Eddie*) Bag of tits.

North-East (*Larry*) All just scaremongery.

Caledonia (*Lenny*) Business as usual.

Cymru (*Curtis*) Don't.

East Midlands (*Donna*) Backhanders . . .

Caledonia (*William*) Rich cunt.

East Midlands (*Donna*) Backhanders again . . .

North-East (*Larry*) Skullduggery.

East Midlands (*Donna*) You do me this favour and I'll do you that favour . . .

South-West (*Eddie*) Blah, blah, blah.

East Midlands (*Donna*) That's not right!

Northern Ireland (*Desmond*) Not OK.

East Midlands (*Donna*) That's not right at all!

Britannia
   They met with a bunch of migrants in Calais
   It's a humanitarian
   love our cake in France
   Project Fear now it's 'Project'
   Brits don't quit
   I rang the official who was actually responsible
      for banning the prawn-cocktail flavoured crisp
   I don't agree
   I agree
   people in this country have had enough of
   They come after you they call you all sorts of things

No
Yes
knickers
cornflakes
Yes
Yes
No
Yes
No no no no no . . .

Cymru (*Curtis*) Don't have any argues.

Caledonia Now listen, Britney –

Britannia
Britannia, my name is Britannia.

I am your memory, your dialects, your cathedrals,
your mosques and markets, schools and pubs,
your woods, mountains, rivers . . .
your motorways and railway lines, your hospitals,
your cenotaphs with paper poppies fading in the rain.

I have breathed you in, like air,
and breathed you out as prayer, or speech, or song.
I am your heartbeat and I take your pulse.
Who else but me can praise your ancient, living
        language as a jewel?
Or trace our wars in raised, ugly scars on her flesh?
Here, Hastings. Here – Bannockburn. Culloden . . .
The welts of Waterloo . . .
Here – the First World War, which culled a generation
        from our shores,
destroyed our future talent, promise, youth –
I count the loss –
and here, World War Two, after only twenty years?
Here – Bloody Sunday. Here – Afghanistan. Iraq.

I sing your thousand musics. I speak your diverse
        poetries.

I am your vital quarrels with yourselves,
your turbulence, your truculence, rage and fear,
your pride, your independence, your despair.
I know your house. Your children. Know your
    ancestors.

We are far more united . . .
We are far more united and have far more in common
    than that which divides us.

Let's hear the votes –

THE FEAST

East Midlands No. We all need a break.

North-East Somethin to eat now, eh? Before the votes,
like.

Cymru Come on now, love? Come on, Britannia.

Northern Ireland Ye're OK, Britannia. It's a tough gig,
sure we all know that.

Cymru It's the Sharing of Food now, eh? You've always
enjoyed that bit. You get to dress up and everything.
(*Sings.*) 'Guide me, O thou great Redeemer . . .'

All sing 'Bread of Heaven' –

All
'Pilgrim through this barren land;
I am weak, but thou art mighty;
Hold me with thy powerful hand:
Bread of heaven, bread of heaven
Feed me till I want no more.
Feed me till I want no more.'

*– while setting out food and attiring and moving
Britannia.*

39

Britannia What are you doing? Put me down!

East Midlands Caledonia? Could you . . .?

Caledonia Of course, aye, aye.
   Ah'd like tae thank Britney, eh, Britannia – on behalf of those able tae be present – for summoning this gathering. The Sharing of Food.

   'Some hae meat and canna eat,
   And some wad eat that want it,
   But we hae meat and we can eat,
   And sae the Lord be thankit.'

Cymru I'm delighted to offer some cawl – and some bara brith.

South-West I present organic Double Gloucester.

Northern Ireland I brought champ . . . mashed potatoes, butter and scallions.

East Midlands I brought Saag Paneer. Also Red Leicester.

Caledonia Ah brought haggis, tattie scones and Talisker. twenty year old.

Cymru Tidy.

North-East Well, in case any of yous was vegetarian like, I brought a Geordie Pizza.

All What's that? (*Etc.*)

North-East It's a pizza base, yeah, with a topping of just chips.

Britannia Thank you, all. Lord be thankit.

All Lord be thankit.

Cymru Cawl, Cariad. Comfort food. In our DNA. Lamb, swede, carrots, potatoes and, most importantly, leeks.

Caledonia Doesn't have it's own poem though. 'Address to a Haggis'.

'Fair fa' yer honest sonsie face,
Great Chieftain o' the pudding-race . . .'

Robert Burns.

All jeer.

Cymru
'To begin at the beginning:
It is Spring, moonless night in the small town . . .'

All jeer.

Oi! That's Dylan Thomas, ya heathens!

Britannia I need a holiday.

Caledonia Parts of Scotland, ye'd have tae go incognito.

Northern Ireland Aye – like, over the water – ye'd need to be careful.

North-East Come to us, pet. Kielder Water and Forest Park has the largest expanse of totally dark sky in the whole of Europe. You can see shootin stars . . . the Milky Way . . . if you're lucky enough you can catch an aurora . . .

South-West Regrettably, the North-East is the binge-drinking capital of the UK . . .

All (*teasing*) Oooh.

North-East *What?*

South-West According to official figures, it has the highest proportion of serial boozers in the country . . .

Caledonia Sad but true.

North-East You can bloody talk.

East Midlands You want to come down Melton Road, Britannia . . . Feast India, Mrs Bridges Tea Rooms . . . diversity . . .

Northern Ireland We do the best parties. We have the largest Halloween celebration *in the world*!

Cymru Bardsey Island! The Island of Twenty Thousand Saints. You can only get there by boat and there's no electricity. Peace. Quiet. Puffins . . .

South-West Regrettably, Newport in Wales has the highest rate of drug trafficking outside London.

All Shocking / Disgraceful.

Cymru Now hang on, boy . . .

South-West Northern Ireland was voted the third worst place to live in the UK –

All Unlucky!

Northern Ireland Are you after a smack in the mouth?

South-West – and East Midlands has the highest rate of teen pregnancies in the country . . .

East Midlands What?

All Shameful!

Caledonia Parts of Scotland you can walk for days and see nothing but deer. No drug traffickers, no pregnant drug traffickers . . . Mebbe an eagle.

South-West Regrettably . . .

Caledonia Don't say it.

South-West Life expectancy . . .

Caledonia I'm warning you . . .

South-West South-West is your best option.

North-East Highest use of marijuana . . .

East Midlands Twenty thousand people using food banks . . .

Northern Ireland Highest annual rainfall . . .

Caledonia And *you*.

North-East At least if you come with us you'll get laid, Britney. We have the most sex.

All No, no / What? / No way.

North-East Fact.

South-West I can vouch for that.

Northern Ireland But my accent was voted sexiest.

North-East Say somethin sexy to us. Go on.

Northern Ireland I don't have to *say something sexy*. It's just the way I talk.

All 'I don't have to say *something sexy*. It's just the way I talk.'

North-East Yer about as sexy as stottie, man.

All 'Yer about as sexy as stottie, man.'

North-East Ah, howayand shite! If it wasn't for the North-East and Joseph Swan, yez wouldna have the light bulb. Ye'd all be sat in the dark.

East Midlands Well, we invented euthanasia.

North-East Ay, well, you'd need that where you're from.

East Midlands And the Salvation Army.

North-East We've got Venerable Bede.

East Midlands And the Quakers.

43

North-East St Cuthbert of the Holy Island at Lindisfarne. Sea otters would crawl out of the North Sea to warm his feet as he prayed.

Northern Ireland St Patrick!

Cymru God!

All God?

Cymru Well I lives in God's country. Tidy.

Caledonia Yiz are all imbeciles. The Scottish people have provided more religious leaders, more engineers, more writers, more footballers, more football *managers*, more comedians, more inventors, more great political figures than the lot o yiz put together.

South-West Tong.

Caledonia *What?*

South-West Tong.

Caledonia What d'ye mean, 'Tong'?

South-West Tong. Tong.

Caledonia Will someone stop him saying 'Tong'?

South-West Tong. On the Isle of Lewis. In the Hebrides. Donald Trump's mother was born there.

Caledonia Donald Trump is not Scottish!

South-West Half-Scottish.

Caledonia Get tae fuck.

All Oooo . . .

South-West Take the pride.

North-East So his mam was Scottish like?

Caledonia Wrong.

East Midlands This is *so* interesting.

Caledonia Wrong.

South-West Mary Anne MacLeod. Spoke Gaelic. Trump's mum.

North-East You mean it was her Mother Tong?

Caledonia Wrong.

South-West Tong, Tong, Tong, Tong.

Cymru Trump's mam was from . . .

All Tong, Tong, Tong, Tong . . .

Northern Ireland The wee Scottish village of . . .

All Tong, Tong, Tong, Tong . . .

Caledonia Right . . .

All Tong, Tong, Tong, Tong . . .

Caledonia That's it.

> *All start singing 'Donald Where's Your Troosers?'*
> *Caledonia interrupts end of first verse.*

I've just got one thing to say to you . . .

> *All continue singing.*

IT'S FAKE NEWS!

> *He exits.*

Britannia It's what I love about him. His independence.

Cymru He's left his bluddy whisky though!

> *All cheer and get the whisky.*

Caledonia Do not . . . Do not touch that whisky.

All Ooh . . .

Caledonia Ah for fuck's sake. But yiz are all in the Last Chance Saloon. (*Pause. Pours whiskies.*) Ye've a face like a yard of gravy.
Slainte!

All Slainte!

Britannia (*glumly*) Slainte.

North-East Come on, man!

Cymru Cheer up, Britney. This is how we do it in the Valleys. Suck on this, Cariad!

> *Music: 'Goldfinger', Riverdance, Propellerheads . . .*
> *'Under the Moon of Love' by Showaddywaddy.*
> *Their revelry is interrupted by Big Ben.*

THE VOTE

Britannia I need to listen to the votes.

Northern Ireland (*Mick*) I voted tae remain.

South-West (*Eddie*) I voted out and so did a lot of people who had the same . . .

East Midlands (*Eric*) We voted to come out. (*Laughs.*)

Caledonia (*Kat*) I did, I did. I voted to remain in the EU.

North-East (*Bill*) I voted out.

South-West (*Leroy*) I wasn't able to vote. But I wanted to –

Cymru (*Curtis*) I'm thirteen years old.

East Midlands (*Donna*) Me and my husband voted out.

Northern Ireland (*Siobhan*) Leave.

South-West (*Mila*) Um . . . Yeah we voted for to stay because like if it was leave we might have to leave.

Cymru (*Paul*) I voted to come out of Europe.

Caledonia (*Glenn*) Remain.

North-East (*Larry*) I voted to leave the EU . . .

South-West (*Jane*) Leave.

North-East (*Larry*) I did, I did vote to leave the EU.

East Midlands (*Panit*) Brexiteer.

Cymru (*Bernice*) Oh, we voted to stay obviously you know but um . . .

Caledonia (*Deirdre*) I voted to remain.

Northern Ireland (*Richard*) We discussed it at home in great detail –

South-West (*Sandra*) I'm a pro-European remainer.

Northern Ireland (*Richard*) – and I made up my mind to vote to stay in Europe.

Caledonia (*William*) I voted for the Brexit, aye, I voted tae stay.

East Midlands (*Julie*) I didn't know who I was gonna vote for until I was in the – the booth.

South-West (*Lottie*) Didn't vote.

East Midlands (*Julie*) And just went, 'You know what, I've got a funny feelin it's gonna go the other way.'

Cymru (*Matthew*) No. I didn't vote. Em . . .

East Midlands (*Julie*) And I decided to stay in.

Northern Ireland (*Sean*) Stay.

Cymru (*Matthew*) I'm anti – em, I don't know –

North-East (*Jude*) Stay.

Cymru (*Matthew*) I didn't think there was point in votin. I really didn't –

Caledonia (*Roseanna*) Remain.

Cymru (*Matthew*) – like – em, I shoulda.

Northern Ireland (*Niamh*) I voted to remain in the EU.

Cymru (*Matthew*) In hindsight, maybe I should've, but I was . . .

North-East (*Barbara*) Remain.

Cymru (*Matthew*) Rebelling against it, I suppose, yeah, in my own sort of way. Em –

South-West (*Stanley*) Frankly, I went for Brexit.

Cymru (*Matthew*) – cos I don't believe votin makes a difference.

Caledonia (*Padma*) I voted remain, solely because I didn't want to be on the side of Farage.

Northern Ireland (*Desmond*) I voted for Brexit.

Cymru (*Angharad*) I voted out. I think I made the wrong decision.

South-West (*Ollie*) I didn't actually vote.

North-East (*Jude*) Leave.

Northern Ireland (*Declan*) I didn't vote – and I feel like an arsehole for it.

East Midlands (*Aravinda*) I voted Brexit.

North-East (*Jasper*) Remain.

South-West (*Donna*) Leave.

East Midlands (*Aravinda*) I thought this would be on majority.

Northern Ireland (*Luke*) I would have voted to stay.

East Midlands (*Aravinda*) Twenty million vs twenty million and one –

South-West (*Ralph*) Remain.

East Midlands (*Aravinda*) You better vote.

Caledonia (*James*) Remain.

Northern Ireland (*Hannah*) Leave.

East Midlands (*Aravinda*) So I did –

Cymru (*Pauline*) Remain.

East Midlands (*Aravinda*) – and I voted Brexit –

North-East (*Roxie*) Remain.

East Midlands (*Aravinda*) – that they should leave.

South-West (*Ralph*) Leave.

Caledonia Leave.

Northern Ireland Leave.

North-East Leave.

South-West Leave.

Cymru Leave.

Britannia (*Farage*) This, if all, if the predictions now are right, this will be a victory for real people, a victory for ordinary people, a victory for decent people.

And today honesty, decency and belief in nation, I think now is going to win.

And we will have done it, we will have done it without having to fight, without a single bullet being fired, we'd have done it by damned hard work on the ground.

Let June 23 go down in our history as our independence day.

Pause.

East Midlands (*Donna*) WOO! I could not believe it

Northern Ireland (*Siobhan*) I was full of fear.

Cymru (*Pauline*) I was absolutely gobsmacked.

South-West (*Eddie*) Really.

Caledonia (*Padma*) I was like, and, and I swear I didn't bother checking till my friend called me.

Northern Ireland (*Siobhan*) She text me being like the sky is falling.

Cymru (*Pauline*) Gobsmacked and frightened.

South-West (*Eddie*) Yep.

Caledonia (*Pauline*) And he was like shit went wrong have you seen it.

South-West (*Eddie*) Really pleased.

Cymru (*Pauline*) I was gobsmacked.

East Midlands (*Donna*) I couldn't sleep all night and I struggled to come down in the morning. And I was afraid to switch on the television. Because I thought it would be remain. And when it said leave –

Caledonia (*Padma*) No, I was like it's remain right, and he was like no it's leave –

East Midlands (*Donna*) Ooh I'm gonna cry in a minute.

Caledonia (*Padma*) Are you ff—?

East Midlands (*Donna*) I shouted up to Joe –

Caledonia (*Padma*) Oh my –

East Midlands (*Donna*) I went Joe, Joe we're leaving! We're leaving!

Cymru (*Pauline*) Gobsmacked.

Caledonia (*Padma*) Like what.

East Midlands (*Donna*) I couldn't believe it.

Caledonia (*Padma*) Are you kidding me.

East Midlands (*Donna*) Och.

Caledonia (Padma) laughs.

I was over the moon.

Caledonia (*Padma*) Then I was like, no –

Northern Ireland (*Niamh*) Listen, I had just got up, I'm sitting here in my pyjamas! I hadn't even had a cup of tea . . . and she was already down here watching the news . . . and I, this, you're a racist, I'm not a racist, you're racist, you know how is that poss— You, you voted for Farage! I said I didn't vote for Farage. I voted to leave the EU, I did not vote for Farage. You did and they told lies! I said, everybody told lies, it was just horrendous.

Cymru (*Pauline*) Gobsmacked.

Pause.

North-East (*Jude*) Right, that's it, end of story, that's what we're gonna do. Get on with it, you know, and that's what I put on Facebook actually, you know (*Laughs.*) And I says right here we are, you know, we don't agree with each other, but never mind you know . . . Just get on with it! It's a democracy.

Britannia (*Cameron*) The country has just taken part in a giant democratic exercise – perhaps the biggest in our history. The British people have voted to leave the European Union and their will must be respected.

I fought this campaign in the only way I know how – which is to say directly and passionately what I think and feel – head, heart and soul.

I held nothing back.

But the British people have made a very clear decision to take a different path, and as such I think the country requires fresh leadership to take it in this direction.

Britannia (*Boris*) I believe David Cameron has been one of the most extraordinary politicians of our age. A brave and principled man, who's given superb leadership of his party and his country.

Britannia (*Gove*) Boris is – an amazing, and an impressive person – but I've realised in the last few days, that Boris isn't capable of building that team and providing that unity, and so I came, reluctantly but firmly to the conclusion, that I had to stand for the leadership of the Conservative Party.

Britannia (*Boris*) I cannot, unfortunately, eh, get on with what I wanted to do, so it'll be up to somebody else now. I wish them every possible success.

Britannia (*Farage*) Isn't it funny? You know, when I came here seventeen years ago, and I said that I wanted to lead a campaign to get Britain to leave the European Union, you all laughed at me. Well, I have to say, you're not laughing now, are you?

Northern Ireland (*Richard*) Eventually this'll become a past history that our children – or children's children –

will read about down and say 'What were they at?' You know? 'Where did that come from?'

East Midlands (*CSO*) So what now? It's awkward isn't it? That – that's very awkward in the place that you're living basically says go home. The country. Not one person. The country.

North-East (*Larry*) A lot of people say, 'Oh we canna dae this, we canna dae that' – well how can't we dae this? We fought in two world wars for God's sake. And we pulled the country back from nothin again. You kna, it was derelict. We pulled the count— pulled the country back from that. Course we can do it again. D-definitely. This – th-this is – this is a great country.

South-West (*Eddie*) Um, and-and it's never all gonna be like, um, you know, love and peace, there'll be some peace but . . . the only way you're gonna get your love is from the brothels.

Interviewer laughs.

Alright, and there's a lack of them in Salisbury, and I think we should have one.

East Midlands (*Panit*) We're not going over a cliff, there is no cliff, we'll carry on, the people have spoken.

Britannia (*Cameron*) Tomorrow I will chair my last cabinet meeting.

South-West (*Lottie*) Legalise weed mate –

Britannia (*Cameron*) On Wednesday I will attend the House of Commons for Prime Minister's Questions.

South-West (*Lottie*) – because, like there is a lot of anger in this world, it is a lot, and people are dying –

Britannia (*Cameron*) After that, er, I expect to go to the Palace and offer my resignation.

South-West (*Lottie*) – a bit of weed, chill, be fine.

Britannia (*Cameron*) So we'll have a new Prime Minister in that building behind me, er, by Wednesday evening.

South-West (*Lottie*) What's with the fighting? 'S no need. Get some bubble gum cush!

Britannia (*Cameron*) Thank you very much. Dee-do-dee-do. Right.

Caledonia (*Lenny*) Ih – it was so fucking preposterous that I, I still cannae quite believe that that is the decision. And then of course the people who fucking well, the cheerleaders for pushing that vote through have disappeared.

Cymru (*Paul*) You got David Cameron. Where's he gone now?

Caledonia (*Lenny*) Oh. Wasn't expecting that. What's your plan? Don't have one. Actually, I'm just gunna get off this bus now, troops. See yas later.

Cymru (*Paul*) I'm going, so long boys. What? I'm going.

North-East (*Barbara*) Now it is worse, much worse there is a very nasty woman as Prime Minister.

East Midlands (*Panit*) I have a lot of faith in . . . in the Prime Minister, a lot of faith.

North-East (*Jude*) I like er, May, she is . . . ah . . . eh honest I hope.

Cymru (*Paul*) I do think Theresa May will be OK.

Caledonia (*Padma*) For me there were two options. Either I was going to be in the hands of EU, or I was going to be in the hands of Tories. Which one do you pick? They're both shit. Now Theresa May, like, nightmare come true. That woman. (*Laughs.*) Oh!

Britannia (*Theresa*) I am honoured and humbled to be chosen by the Conservative Party to become its leader.

South-West (*Beryl*) I think Theresa May will make a good Maggie Thatcher.

Britannia (*Theresa*) Brexit means Brexit and we're going to make a success of it.

South-West (*Beryl*) I wish she'd wear her clothes longer, her skirts. Either go for it – and her jackets. Her jackets are too short –

Britannia (*Theresa*) We need a strong, new, positive vision for the future of our country, a vision of a country that works not for the privileged few but that works for every one of us.

South-West (*Beryl*) Everybody's said her shoes is nice, but – that's immaterial to me. I gotta wear like trainers, cos my leg's like . . . yeah.

Britannia (*Theresa*) Come with me, and together, let's seize the day!

Caledonia (*Padma*) That term – Bres— Brexit means Brexit. (*Laughs.*) Like – (*Laughs.*) Explain Brexit. It means Brexit. Yeah I'll take a note of that. What the fuck.

THE LEAVE-TAKING

Northern Ireland (*Richard*) No, so, no – I would be very much a point of – I'm not a looker-backer. And I know there's not such a – such a word or a phrase but . . . I want to look forward all the time. I can't – Yesterday was yesterday. I had a nice day yesterday. But it's gone! You know. It's gone . . . ahh maybe not.

North-East (*Bill*) Last night I felt more British than I'd ever felt. We were in a damp shed, brewing tea, pouring down rain, freezing cold. Committed to a project that is far too complicated for wa. That, that to me is Britishness.

From here on, gradually the regions put their ballot boxes on their chairs, take their coats and briefcases and leave.

South-West (*Jane*) I hate to think that we've left the world in a mess, no we haven't left the world in a mess, you know, we are lucky, we are the lucky ones we come down every morning and we've had a good night's sleep, we switch on the tap and beautiful water comes out . . . (*Drifts into audio.*) So many people in the world don't have that, so, sometimes I wish we would count our blessings and be grateful for what we have got, you know it's the old, old adage, don't wish for what you've not got, be thankful for what you have got.

But as I say I'm a cock-eyed optimist (*Laughs.*) I sometimes think this country could do with a benign dictator and I'm the one to do it!

East Midlands (*Avarinda*) I think future will be bright. And I think... an – that this country has been going down and down and down.

They are great . . . (*Drifts into audio.*) And they will be great again. Not that they'll be ruling the world again, but . . . they'll be living bit better than . . . not something for nothing, only something for those who deserve it.

Cymru (*Bernice*) March or April a letter came through the door and it had like a royal seal on the back of it. My husband he's a bit of a practical joker and he can do letters and send 'em off and people will think that it's a genuine letter you know and he's done things like tell people their microwaves will blow up or their toilet is gonna be off or whatever, so anyway I ripped it open and said . . . (*Drifts into audio.*) Oh my God, I said, I've been nominated for an award in the Birthday Honours . . . and I looked at him and I said right, where've you had this from? He said it's nothing to do with me, I said it's for services to education. Well you better ring somebody in the school, he said, ring Margaret. So I rang her first . . .

Only the voices remain (audio) and Britannia.

Caledonia (*William*) When I used to go to school, we'd look at . . . Fettes over the road, wi' its massive sweepin driveway . . . and the castle that we used to call Castle Duckula . . . You know fae the show? *Count Duckula,* yeah?

North-East (*Barbara*) Well, I was actually born on a farm er, in, er, at Ottercaps which is just down from Otterburn er, so it, my dad was a tenant farmer . . . and I just from day one I loved the farm really so . . . er . . . and so I followed my dad about when I could!

Northern Ireland (*Richard*) I love the British connection, the tradition, but I'm not a big Queen person. Nobody wants us. They've only held on to us because they know no one else wants us.

East Midlands (*Donna*) Um, you don't sort of see enough of your own people, OK, yes, I'm in the wrong area but it would be nice just to see some of your own people more often than you see of other races. Whereas if you go down to the seaside or go down south or somethin' you know, then you're with your own a bit more.

Cymru (*Curtis*) Curtis Thomas Popp. Thirteen years old. I live in Merthyr Tydfil and I was born in 2003 and that's it. I wanna support my country. Oh it's amazing, you sh— should um . . . you should come and ave, er . . . a look at the sights. You get good . . . you get good people running stores, you get good friends here, you get good schools, you get good . . . train service, you get good bus service, you get, um, good taxi service. Yooooou get good town, you get good sh— you get good shopping centres . . .

Britannia I have loved you all for ever. You children of these changing, feisty, funny, generous islands. The seeds of our circumstances flower into our actions. We cannot stand in judgement on each other's lives. But we should seek and search and strive for good leadership. Are you listening? Do I hear you listening?

End.